D1462064

Published by Creative Education and
Creative Paperbacks
P.O. Box 227, Mankato, Minnesota 56002
Creative Education and Creative Paperbacks
are imprints of The Creative Company
www.thecreativecompany.us

Design by The Design Lab
Production by Chelsey Luther
Printed in the United States of America

Photographs by Alamy (Steve Bloom Images), Corbis
(Theo Allofs, Tui De Roy/Minden Pictures),
Dreamstime (Arjenschippers, Isselee), Getty Images
(Tom Vezo), iStockphoto (AwakenedEye), News-
com (FEDERICO GAMBARINI/AFP/Getty Images),
Shutterstock (kavram, Sergio Martinez), SuperStock
(Biosphoto, NHPA)

Copyright © 2015 Creative Education,
Creative Paperbacks
International copyright reserved in all countries. No
part of this book may be reproduced in any form
without written permission from the publisher.

Library of Congress Cataloging-in-Publication Data
Riggs, Kate.
Vultures / Kate Riggs.
p. cm. — (Amazing animals)
Summary: A basic exploration of the appearance,
behavior, and habitat of vultures, the carrion-eating
birds of prey. Also included is a story from folklore
explaining why vultures are bald.
Includes index.
ISBN 978-1-60818-492-7 (hardcover)
ISBN 978-1-62832-092-3 (pbk)
1. Vultures—Juvenile literature. 2. Scavengers (Zool-
ogy)—Juvenile literature. 3. Ecology—Juvenile literature. I. Title. II. Series: Amazing animals.
QL696.F32R547 2015
598.9'4—dc23   2013051253

CCSS: RI.1.1, 2, 4, 5, 6, 7; RI.2.2, 5, 6, 7, 10;
RI.3.1, 5, 7, 8; RF.1.1, 3, 4; RF.2.3, 4

First Edition
9 8 7 6 5 4 3 2 1

3 1526 04789778 7

AMAZING ANIMALS
VULTURES

BY KATE RIGGS

CREATIVE EDUCATION · CREATIVE PAPERBACKS

Vultures belong to a group of birds known as raptors. Old World vultures live in Europe, Asia, and Africa. New World vultures live in the Americas. Turkey vultures are the most common kind of New World vultures.

The turkey vulture's wrinkly, red head makes it recognizable

Vultures have feathers everywhere except their faces. Their beaks are hooked. The most colorful parts of vultures are their heads. Many vultures have red, pink, yellow, white, or black faces.

A vulture's beak is made of keratin (like human fingernails)

Andean condors live in the Andes Mountains of South America

The cinereous (*sih-NIH-ree-us*) vulture is one of the world's largest raptors. It can weigh up to 31 pounds (14 kg). Hooded vultures are much smaller. They weigh about three to six pounds (1.4–2.7 kg). Andean condors have the largest **wingspan**. Their wings stretch 10.5 feet (3.2 m) across.

wingspan how far it is from one wingtip to the other

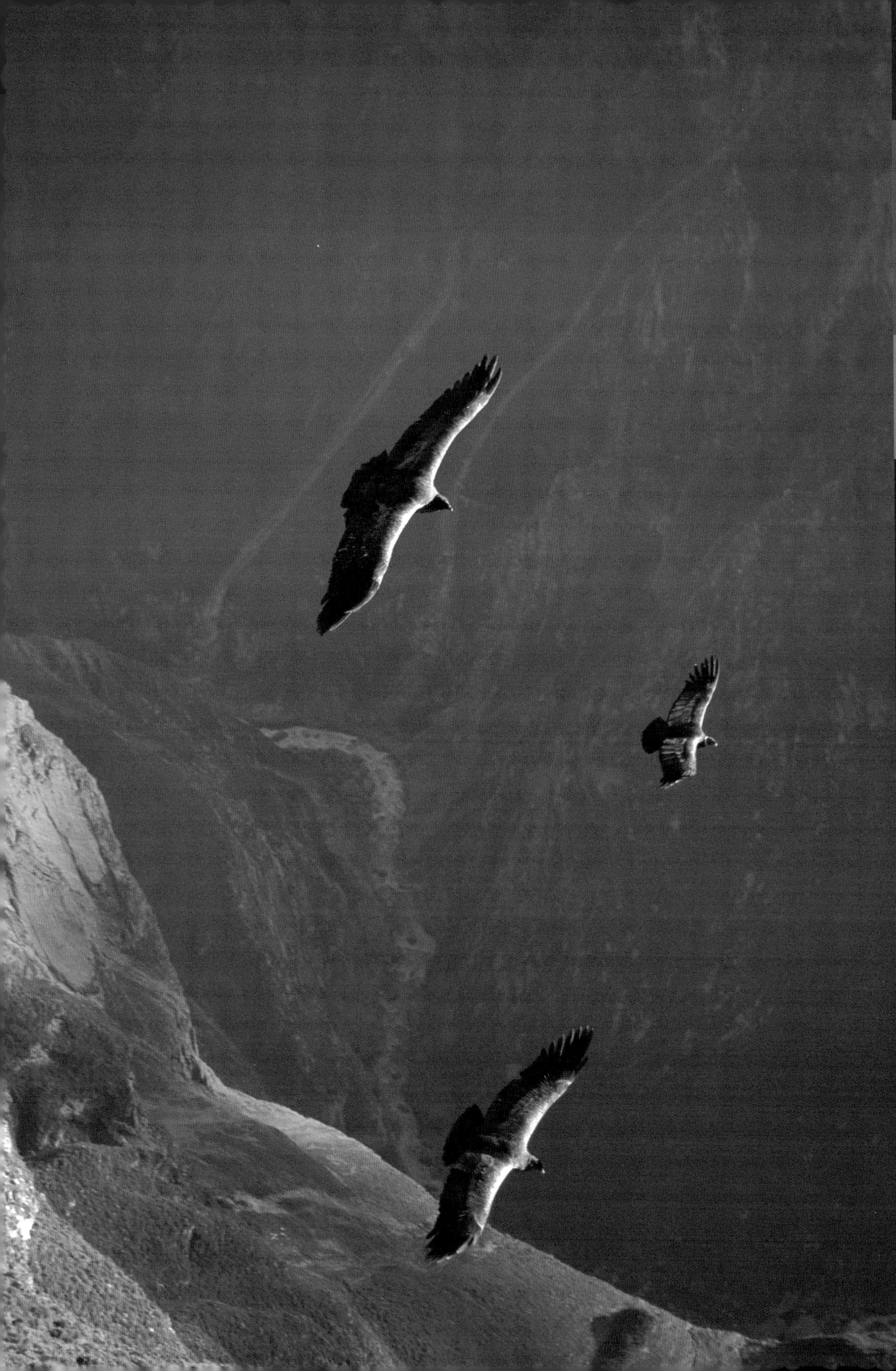

New World vultures have shorter legs than Old World vultures. But Old World vultures have sharper claws called talons. Vultures have good eyesight. They also have an excellent sense of smell.

Vultures can use their talons to help them land on rocky cliffs

Vultures can smell or see food as they fly high above the ground. Vultures are called scavengers because they eat animals that are already dead. A vulture uses its beak like a knife to cut into meat.

Scavengers like vultures are nature's way of keeping places clean

Baby vultures do not have the same coloration as adults

Vultures begin their life inside eggs. The mother and father take turns keeping the eggs warm. **Chicks** come out of the eggs in 30 to 70 days. They fight over food. Young vultures leave the nest after they learn how to fly.

chicks baby vultures

Ruppell's griffon vultures can live for 40 to 50 years in Africa

Vultures do not have many predators. Many kinds of vultures can live for 25 years in the wild. A turkey vulture named Toulouse (*too-LOOZ*) lived at a zoo for more than 40 years!

predators animals that kill and eat other animals

Vultures search for food in the daytime. They fly in circles or sit in a tall tree. They group together to tear meat apart. They eat and eat until they are full.

Vultures can eat 20 percent of their body weight in one sitting

Vultures fly high in warm pockets of air called thermals

Some vultures are common around the world. People can see them in forests or **deserts**. Other times, people go to zoos to see these bald birds!

deserts hot, dry lands with little rainfall

VULTURES

A Vulture Story

Why is the vulture bald? People in Africa told a story about this. Long ago, an angry god who lived near the sun would not let it rain. So the most beautiful bird in the world flew to the sun. The heat burned the feathers off her head. When the god saw how much she had suffered, he let the rain come down. But the bird—the vulture— is bald to this day.

Read More

O'Neill, Amanda. *I Wonder Why Vultures Are Bald, and Other Questions about Birds*. New York: Kingfisher, 1997.

Sayre, April Pulley. *Vulture View*. New York: Henry Holt, 2007.

Websites

DLTK's Letter V Crafts for Kids
http://www.dltk-teach.com/alphabuddies/letter-v.html
This page will take you to vulture crafts you can make.

Idaho Public Television: Birds of Prey
http://idahoptv.org/dialogue4kids/season5/boprey/birdpreyfact.cfm
Learn about vultures and other birds of prey.

Note: Every effort has been made to ensure that the websites listed above are suitable for children, that they have educational value, and that they contain no inappropriate material. However, because of the nature of the Internet, it is impossible to guarantee that these sites will remain active indefinitely or that their contents will not be altered.

Index